Start Your Own Business Today!

Your Guide to Investing in a Business with Guaranteed Success

By: Jeff White

9781635014297

I0510871

PUBLISHERS NOTES

Disclaimer – Speedy Publishing LLC

Speedy Publishing LLC

40 E Main Street, Newark, Delaware, 19711

Contact Us: 1-888-248-4521

Website: http://www.speedypublishing.co

REPRINTED Paperback Edition: 9781635014297:

Manufactured in the United States of America

DEDICATION

To Leah, my baby girl. You bring the sun with you everywhere you go.

TABLE OF CONTENTS

CHAPTER 1- THE JOYS OF HAVING YOUR OWN BUSINESS

Starting a home-based business is an exciting and rewarding adventure. No longer must you deal with inner office politics, work hard to please a boss or stay in line with co-workers. And never again will you have to suffer the long commute, as you'll wake up in your place of business! But there's a more important reason to consider developing your very own home based business.

With the shaky economy and thousands of people out of jobs without notice, creating your home-based business can provide you with the stability you've been searching for. You will be in control of your own financial future, be able to make decisions for yourself and spend time building a business that can withstand economic changes, as well as the test of time. For many, building a home-based business remains a far-fetched dream, as they believe that it's not only costly, but a risky endeavor.

The truth is however, that if you focus on building a business within an evergreen market, where customers will consistently purchase your goods and services despite economic changes, you will never have to worry about whether your business has what it takes to survive. Imagine the possibilities of being able to dedicate yourself to building a profitable business. Every hour you put into it goes towards solidifying an asset that belongs entirely to you.

No more late night shifts where you're barely able to pay the bills, and never again will you be working to build someone else's financial future, but instead, you'll be focused on working for the one person who truly matters - yourself!

The Secrets to a Successful Business

The most underappreciated investment is easy to find. We all see it each and every day. Most likely we believe that we are paying attention to it and treating it fairly well. If the suspense has gotten to you let me tell you what the answer is. The answer is you. You are most likely your most underappreciated investment. Investing takes a combination of time, money, and passion. Do you truly devote yourself to those three things? If you don't it is time to start doing so.

Time

As busy people we all need time. Investing takes time. Reflect back on all the things that you are curious about or would like to know more about. Have you actively tried to quench your thirst for knowledge in those areas? If you have not you should take the time to do so. For example, if you are interested in investing in only green investments you should understand the basic principles and specific differences of green investing compared to other types of investing.

Money

Most all investments do involve money or at least a request for money. It would be fantastic if you could be prosperous and thrive for an investment that just required your time and brain power. The chances are slim. So, while you are waiting for that to come along you should find ways to generate the money you need to invest in what you desire. For many people this means higher education so opportunities for higher pay open up. People are driven by what improving them can do for themselves and those they love.

Passion

When a person is passionate about something it is usually all consuming in the most positive of ways. You talk about it with energy and become a natural sales person. You think about it more than just about anything else. You also try to find out how to make that happen. If you need to get others to invest in your vision they will screen you fairly heavily. The more you've invested in yourself through education and knowledge the better your chances are of finding people to join in.

Don't underestimate or neglect one of the most major investments you can make. That is the investment in you. When you give yourself time, figure out how to make more money, and pursue your passions you will have found a winning combination for an investment you can monitor 24/7.

Encourage Others to Invest in Your Business

If you have a dream and vision for owning your own business you also have a lot of work to do to make that dream become your reality. There are three main things that you need to have in place in order to make it all happen. You need a solid business plan, you need specific goals and objectives, and you need make sure that people will want whatever service your business offers.

The Solid Business Plan

A solid business plan takes time to write. Many times people work on business plans for a year before they are set to go. Some of the critical components to a solid business plan are break even points, detailed description of services, back-up plans for adjustments, and the financial management of the plan. Only when you have that business plan completed should you start investing money into your business or approach anybody else about investing in it. If you go to a bank they will listen, give some advice, and tell you to come back when a solid business plan is in place. If you are considering family members and friends for financing they deserve the same professionalism from you that the bank demands.

Specific Goals and Objectives

The business plan will help lay out some of this but understanding your specific goals and objectives is really where the passion comes in. Owning your own business is definitely two things in the beginning – exciting and a lot of work. You need to understand your intentions and reasons for diving in. When you do the rest will fall into place much easier.

Make Sure People Need Your Business

If you want your business to be your fulltime income and livelihood it is a good idea to make sure that people need what you are providing. If they don't or the market is very small it is really more like a profitable hobby. That is okay too. Just make sure that you don't confuse the two. You also need to clarify that your costs are in-line with competitors in your area of service. When you are starting your own business you need to be up to the challenge. You need a solid business plan, specific goals and objectives, and a business service that people need. If you have all that you have the solid foundation you need to help it all come together.

Chapter 2- Businesses That You Can Start Almost Immediately! (No Equipment Needed)

• **Bookkeeping Business Service**

With a bookkeeping business, you'll have no shortage of potential clients as so many people dislike bookkeeping and are willing to hire a professional to take care of it for them. Better yet, bookkeeping services are always in demand, even in a shaky economy, as businesses require additional help managing their finances and evaluating budgets.

Successful bookkeepers need to be reliable, precise, thorough and willing to review their work for accuracy. Your clients will depend on you and so you'll need to be willing to commit yourself to fulfilling your obligations, and in taking great care to handle their business and personal bookkeeping with the upmost professionalism.

In order to set up a home based bookkeeping service, you will need to be experienced in accounting and utilizing spreadsheet software, so this business is best suited for those who have had previous experience working in financial and accounting departments for companies or employers.

If you don't have the experience needed, you could consider taking a short-term accounting course through your local community college. You could also take a distance training course from hoe through online colleges and training facilities to gain the knowledge and experience needed to run a successful bookkeeping business. I recommend purchasing "QuickBooks Pro" (retail $200-$240) which is the most popular accounting software on the market today and also the easiest to use, even if you have no experience bookkeeping.

The overall profits of a bookkeeping service are absolutely phenomenal as your startup costs and business operation costs are minimal once you have the software and management tools that you need. You can expect to earn anywhere between $30-$50 per hour based on the services you offer and the types of clients you accept.

In order to determine your price structure, you will want to evaluate existing bookkeeping services in your area, as well as the level of work you do, ranging from basic book keeping to extensive preparation of financial statements and business accounts.

Bookkeepers often include tax returns in their service listing each year as a way of making extra money on a seasonal basis.

Start Your Own Business Today!

A great way to get started in bookkeeping is by targeting brand new businesses. There are over 500,000 new start-ups each year within the United States alone and many of these people require help in managing and maintaining their business records, because they are new to the world of commerce!

Consider targeting these start-up businesses by offering them an overview of the services you offer, along with your business card.

If you have experience and training, you will want to highlight that on your service sheet by attaching a "Credentials" page to the pamphlet.

A home-based bookkeeping business carries a very low startup cost. In fact, you can build your business for less than $1,000, and if you already own a personal computer and accounting software, your costs are tremendously cut down even more!

In fact, all you will really need is a business registration unless you intend to do business using your own name.

Other benefits of a home-based bookkeeping business include:

- No zoning requirements

Since you will be completing your work from your home office, there is no traffic to and from your home, eliminating the need for business zoning or licensing.

- No Special Equipment Needed

Other than a personal PC, accounting software and a fax machine, there is little involved or needed in starting a home based bookkeeping service.

- Work on the Side

Many bookkeepers start their business to supplement their existing income, and since you can set your own hours and take on only a few clients, this business is something you can do while keeping your full time job.

- No Inventory

You never have to purchase, manage or maintain inventory reducing your expenses and eliminating overhead!

- **Medical Billing Service**

As a medical billing specialist, you'll be responsible for issuing invoices on behalf of a physical or medical office. In many cases, doctors struggle to get paid by patients or insurers and it would be your job to secure payment on their behalf.

Your job may also include mailing patient statements, entering in patient information into online databases, posting payments, and handling billing inquiries and even following up on all unpaid invoices.

As a medical billing specialist, your tasks will also include submitting invoices online, including sending insurance claims directly to the insurance companies such as Medicare.

Since insurance agencies give priority to claims filed electronically, you can maximize your ability to secure payment for your clients while minimizing your workload through eliminating the need to personally mail invoices or collect payment.

Start Your Own Business Today!

There are very few skills required in order to start a home based medical billing business, however you will want to brush up on medical terminology so that you understand the different references made within the medical industry.

You will also be required to use medical terminology if you offer extended services that include completing patient records or explaining to patients what the invoice involves.

You will want to learn the basic medical billing and claim process as well, such as how to bill patients and insurance companies, how to file claims, follow up with invoices and how to report diagnoses and trace claims.

The key to building a successful home based medical billing business is to build relationships with your clients so that you can gain the trust and confidence needed to secure projects over a long term period.

Billing is incredibly important to doctors and they'll rely on you to make sure they are paid for services rendered, so you need to demonstrate your ability to effectively follow claims and follow up on a regular basis.

To get started, you will want to develop a business plan that highlights your road to success. Include the tools and resources you need any training or resource sites that you can use to expand your knowledge, and how you plan to market and manage your business.

Through careful planning and preparation you will be able to build a viable business set up for long term success.

You will also want to choose the type of business that is most appropriate based on your marketing outreach and client base. You can register a business as either a sole proprietorship, as a partnership or even a LLC (Limited Liability Company), and later expand your business into a Corporation.

It's important to understand the differences between each business license so that you are fully protected, so contact your local business center for assistance before registering your business.

You also need to make sure that you have any required permits or registration requirements taken care of before you begin to secure clients While it's unlikely that you'll need to obtain any special licensing to run a home based medical billing business, it's always best to be fully prepared by talking with a small business specialist.

As for setting up shop, you'll require very little other than a computer, fax machine, HCFA 1500 forms, additional phone line dedicated to your business, office supplies and the most important tool, your medical billing software.

Medical billing software can run anywhere between $200-$500, depending on the features and flexibility of the software application, so make sure to research different software options before purchasing.

In addition, whenever possible ask for a demo of the software prior to purchase so that you can personally evaluate the software paying attention to ease of use and available features. You want to purchase software that can grow as your business does; avoiding unnecessary expenses later on if you are required to purchase upgrades or additional software components. Make sure that the software developers are willing to provide training and support should you encounter problems with the software, or need additional help learning how it works. Startup costs should not exceed $2000, depending on the resources and equipment you already have, as well as the extent of the services you plan to offer.

Marketing your home-based medical billing business is important in order to secure enough clients to maintain your business. You can market your business a number of different ways, including by contacting local doctors and medical centers offering your assistance. Ask for referrals from doctors that may know other physicians that are looking for a personal medical billing specialist and always be on the lookout for ways of maximizing your business exposure through local business centers and advertising channels.

You could also create an introductory packet that includes your business card as well as a summary of your services and distribute it directly to medical centers and physicians in your local area. And don't forget, you can also offer your services to doctors in other areas as well, by advertising your service online! Join the Chamber of Commerce for additional business support and direct referrals, and consider finding a business mentor to help guide you along.

And finally, continue learning about the medical billing industry. The more you know about it, the more you work towards networking with others who are experience in the business and the more you work towards building brand awareness, the easier it will be to secure clients and building a profitable and long term business of your own!

• **Medical Transcription Service**

Medical transcription is an exciting career. Not only can you work from the comfort of your own home, but you can consistently advance your training to open up the doors to new opportunities, including building your own home based MT business. For the most part, medical transcriptionists will be responsible for converting patient records and medical files into typewritten documents, rather than handwritten to avoid misinterpretation.

All transcripts must be grammatically correct and free of errors as the medical industry requires specific guidelines be met when transcribing audio files into patient records.

The medical transcription industry does not require training or specific accreditation in order to secure employment, however the majority of new transcriptionists seek out online training as a method of gaining hands-on training and experience prior to entering the job market. Not only will training help equip you with the knowledge you need, but it will also provide you with specific skills necessary in the MT job market, including typing, processing, and medical terminology.

Here are some of the things every medical transcriptionist needs to know (and is trained to understand via a MT course):

• Knowledge of disease processes

• Knowledge of anatomy and physiology

• Basic understanding of medical terminology and punctuation used

• Above average typing skills

• Ability to work independently, taking direction.

• Knowledge of medical writing style, and overall grammar.

• Ability to work with audio recordings, voice manipulations and translation.

When it comes to medical transcription, there are a few things you will need to equip your office with in order to be able to complete projects for hospitals and physicians. To start, you will want to purchase word processing software, such as MS Word or WordPerfect. Make sure that you install and configure your word processing software so that you are familiar with the settings, and if possible, learn to use macros which will help automate repetitive tasks, speeding up your productivity.

You will also need a transcriber machine in the event your clients are using dictation tapes when creating their audio files. Transcriber machines play back audiotape files making it possible for you to transcribe and translate as you listen to the recording.

Transcriber machines also offer the ability to slow down the speed so that you can keep the pace as you type, as well as offer "stop points", where you can temporarily pause the audio at a specific point to return to it later on.

These days, you can usually purchase transcriber machines that will effectively play multiple size recording tapes, however depending on the size of the tapes that your clients use; you may need to purchase multiple transcriber machines.

Certain clients will request that they dictate via the telephone and in those cases, you will want to look into setting up a voice system line that will compress voice files so you can transfer them to your computer.

Other equipment that may be required can include a copy machine, fax machine, dedicated phone lines, email addresses, FTP client to upload and download files, and printer.

There are an incredible number of MT jobs available, and with health care facilities continuing to expand, the number of medical transcription jobs available in the market continue to multiply as well.

There are however, different variations of the MT job opportunity with in-house positions being offered (where you work at the physician's office or directly in the hospital) as well as telecommuting based positions, where you are able to work from home on your own schedule.

One thing to keep in mind is that when you work as a MT freelancer, you are responsible for your own taxes and are not offered the same employee benefits, as you would be if you worked directly for a company, on-site. In addition, pay scales will also vary, depending on the amount of work you take on and the actual company or doctor hiring you to complete their projects.

For the most part, MT opportunities offer very lucrative pay options, ranging anywhere from $12-25.00 per hour. You can also choose to take on projects that pay per line, rather than per project, although the majority of online companies and employees hiring telecommuting based freelancers seem to prefer a "per project" basis.

Another incredibly beneficial aspect of becoming a medical transcriptionist is in your ability to consistently expand your business, eventually offering MT training yourself, consulting, coaching and online-courses.

Start Your Own Business Today!

You could make money providing personal help to new medical transcriptionists, or in building a freelance team of MTs where you are responsible for managing incoming projects and client requests.

The world of medical transcription is a profitable and exciting one, and can be very rewarding if you have been interested in becoming a home based worker, or in building a business of your own. One of the easiest ways to land projects is by signing up to medical transcription community forums, and job boards where you will be able to communicate with other MT professionals, as well as keep a pulse on upcoming job offers and opportunities.

You will also want to create a resume that showcases your skillsets, experiences and abilities and upload it to the Internet so that's accessible to potential clients who may want to evaluate your overall potential.

As you become an experienced medical transcriptionist, it's likely that you will reach a point where you are receiving more client requests and project offers than you can handle. When this happens, it's time to consider expanding your business by developing your own freelance team of MT professionals.

Outsourcing work to medical transcriptionists is easy. You don't have to worry about in-house meetings, rent out office space, health benefits or even employment benefits. You can easily form a complete team of MT freelancers in a matter of days just by following a very simple strategy.

Be very specific with the types of projects you are offering so that those interested in bidding on your projects are aware of your expectations, minimizing wasted time responding to applicants with no real knowledge of the industry.

When you find a few freelancers that you are interested in, consider setting up an online interview prior to hiring them.

Ask them a series of questions relating to medical transcription, review work references, and spend some time communicating with each potential applicant so that you can get a good feel as to whether they are a good fit for your newly found team.

When it comes to payment, consider paying them in a similar way that you are used to being paid, either by project, or by line. You will also have to consider offering payment so that you are able to generate a profit from each project you outsource.

For example, you could offer them a few cents less per line than your clients are paying you. After all, you will still have to proof read their work prior to submitting it to your client.

Apart from online freelance marketplaces, one of the easiest methods of finding trustworthy, reliable transcriptionists is by contacting online courses and offering placement for new graduates, or by contacting your local community college or training program and offering jobs to new members.

Not only will you be able to hire medical transcriptionists at lower rates than you would more seasoned freelancers, but you are directly helping them gain hands-on experience necessary for them to eventually go out on their own.

• **Wholesale and Auction Business**

Online auctions are places where you sell items to the highest bidder via a community style marketplace. It works just as a real auction. A product is showcased to the audience and its features and benefits are highlighted, giving potential buyers the chance to bid on the listing or in some cases, to purchase it instantly via a BIN (buy it now) button.

You could easily become a member of an auction site and buy and sell products for a profit either by selling products you already have, products you can create (scrapbook layouts, crafts, etc.), or by purchasing products through a wholesale or drop shipping service who will handle all delivery and fulfillment on your behalf.

Those who sell consistently via online auction sites are referred to as "powersellers" and are able to build very profitable businesses online while establishing credibility within auction marketplaces. Becoming a powerseller is relatively easy if you are committed to consistently researching new markets, evaluating what products are in demand and adjusting your product inventory to satisfy overall demand, keeping in mind that what is popular today can quickly change tomorrow. There are really only a few things that you need to become a powerseller on marketplaces like eBay:

• Quality (popular) products to sell

• A digital camera so that you can take pictures of the items that you're selling.

• A computer

• The enthusiasm to become an eBay powerseller and increase your annual income

You'll want to make sure that you have enough room in your house to accommodate the items that you're going to be selling. You'll need to have room set aside not only to store these items but also a space set aside where you can manage the shipping of these items.

Getting started selling at eBay is as simple as registering your name, or your business name. There are some details that you'll need to include in your registration as a seller, such as where you are located and how you plan on shipping your sold items.

Your goal as an eBay powerseller should be to look as professional as you can so that buyers take you seriously and learn to trust your reputation. Setting up an "online" shop is one way that you can gain a more professional outlook among the many sellers that can be found on eBay.

There are several different options available at eBay that will help you to make a good impression on buyers. You don't want buyers to think of you as just another eBay seller and pass you by for a more professional seller.

When you first start selling your items on eBay you'll find that there is a learning curve as you find out what works for you and what doesn't. The important thing is to be flexible so that you can make changes to the way that you sell in your favor.

Getting Started

There are many benefits to selling on eBay. Some of these legal and financial benefits include:

• The low cost of registering at eBay.

• The ability to have fast and secure transactions with your buyers.

• Tax laws that are clearly defined.

• Accounting advice that even an amateur can follow.

• Low advertising costs.

• Free advertising tools.

The first thing that you will have to do in order to sell on eBay to is register. There are several reasons why you first have to register on eBay. These include:

• EBay requires a certain amount of personal information from you. This is to keep the eBay site secure.

• EBay requires that you register with them before you can begin selling an item or bidding on other saleable items.

• Registration will provide you with updates on the latest eBay information and deals.

You will be required to provide your name, address, phone number, and a valid e-mail address. Many eBay powersellers choose to use a business name for their online transactions. You'll want to include this business name in your eBay registration.

The next step needed for registration is your online user ID. This is the ID by which you will be known as both a buyer and seller.

Make sure to choose an ID name that sounds businesslike and professional. There are some simple basics that you should know about listing your items for sale on eBay. The more items that you list the more experienced you'll become in knowing how to write descriptions to entice buyers to take a longer look at the item that you're selling than the items of other sellers.

The first thing that you need to do is find items that you want to sell. For your first few selling attempts choose items that you yourself like so that you can create a listing that you can relate to.

Find similar items that are for sale on eBay so that you get a good idea of how much the item is worth, what other sellers are selling it for, and what category it best fits into. To find items that are similar to the one that you're selling use the following steps:

• Use the "Search" button at the top of the eBay webpage.

• Select the "Advanced Search" and type in key search words.

• Choose the "Completed Items Only" option.

You'll quickly have a listing of items that were for sale on eBay but are now ended so that you can see what items are popular and what didn't sell.

Once you have your item ready to sell you're ready to begin listing it. The steps that you'll need to complete, in the following order, are:

• Select the format that you want to use to sell your item.

• Choose the best category for the item.

• Write a title that catches the eye of buyers.

• Write a complete description of the item making sure to include all the specifics such as measurements and condition.

• Include photos of the item that you're selling in the listing.

- Let buyers know where you live.

- Use some of the promotion tools available at eBay to promote the item.

- Include the payment that you'll accept for the item as well as information about shipping and packaging.

Be creative and step outside of the box. You need to establish new ways of marketing the items that you're selling. Take time to examine your competitors on eBay so that you know what they're doing and what you have to do better.

Chapter 3- Businesses That You Can Start Almost Immediately! (Some Equipment Required)

- **Home-Based Cleaning Service**

Starting a home based cleaning service is not only affordable, but requires very little set up time, as you can develop a series of services for your local area, purchase supplies and set up shop in a matter of a few short weeks. With busy parents struggling to keep their homes tidy, to the elderly who need a bit of extra help around the house and garden; you could easily tap into an ever growing market right in your local area.

Start Your Own Business Today!

In regards to the legalities of starting a home based cleaning business, you'll want to consider getting licensed and properly bonded. This provides customers with assurance that you are a professional, and will provide them with the protection they need. After all, odds are that you'll be in their homes while they aren't present.

You also have two primary options when setting up your home based cleaning service. You can choose to cater exclusively to residential areas or include commercial properties in your marketing message.

Keep in mind that in order to service commercial areas you will require bonding and additional insurance (along with licensing depending on your local area, as well as individual commercial requirements including security clearances and personal security checks).

The commercial arena is usually far more competitive than residential with larger cleaning services catering to businesses, so you might want to consider targeting residential areas first, and later when you've gained experience, expanding your service to include businesses and retail outlets.

The equipment needed for a home based cleaning service will vary, depending on the types of services you are willing to provide. You will need an industry grade vacuum cleaner, dust clothes, mops and cleaning clothes to get started, but you should also consider the different types of polishes and cleaners available to you.

Many people aren't fond of strong, scented cleaners being used in their homes due to how abrasive these cleaners are on furniture, but another thing to keep in mind is whether there are people with allergies in the home.

An alternative is to purchase "green" cleaners that are both effective at cleaning even the toughest spots, but also environmentally friendly to both pets and animals. You can also use this to your advantage via your marketing message as well, by highlighting the fact that you only work with all natural, toxin free cleaners, so potential clients are given extra incentive to hire you.

As for your service list, you could start off with a basic service listing that includes common cleaning services such as:

- Washing Floors, Sweeping
- Dusting
- Washing Windows
- Replacing light bulbs
- Washing Walls
- Vacuuming
- Waxing Floors
- Cleaning specific rooms (bathrooms, attics, organizing, removing trash, etc.)

And you can later extend your services to include all of the little things like laundry, dishes, making beds and even a bit of yard work.

One of the most important aspects of developing a home-based cleaning business involves careful planning.

You want to write down your ideas, including the types of services you are interested in offering and thoroughly evaluate all options, including how much time it will take per household to fulfill your obligations. Since it's likely that you will start out on your own without the help of a team, you will want to be careful with the number of clients you take on, so that you can spend the needed time on each client's home without ending up overwhelmed.

As someone who has operated a home based cleaning service for many years, I recommend taking on 2-4 clients, getting a feel for what the business involves and then slowly grow your business to include additional clients. It's important that each client is fully satisfied so that they refer other people to you, and you want to be able to retain your clients over a long period of time, so give each client the attention they deserve and take it one day at a time!

As your business grows, you can then expand your service offer as well as consider hiring help, creating a professional home cleaning team for your local area that offers a wide variety of services at affordable rates.

It's also important to spend time evaluating existing competition, so that you are able to determine what price range is acceptable, so you can stay competitive.

Depending on the level of competition in your area, you can expect to earn up to $50 per hour based on the services you provide and the number of clients you take on.

You can also offer to clean homes on a "per project" basis, where your clients pay a weekly fee for a series of cleaning options, or for larger homes, you could charge on an hourly basis, billing clients each week for services rendered.

Tip: When evaluating your price structure, make sure to calculate the costs of cleaners and supplies, as well as the cost to travel to each client's residence!

In order to properly manage your business, you will want to purchase a home computer along with a database and invoice program such as Excel.

This way, you can keep on top of what each client is interested in, as well as develop an organized system and schedule to help you stay focused. Your clients will expect to receive an invoice and a receipt for your cleaning services so make sure to purchase paper stock, a printer, ink, and a program to help you create and maintain invoices for future reference.

One of the best ways of to build a successful home based cleaning service is to choose a specific niche market and cater to it. For example, there are different categories of clients involved in offering residential cleaning, including:

• Senior homes
• Family homes
• Single person homes (bachelors, etc.)
• Daycares

Creating your cleaning business so it's tailored towards a specific segment of the market will help you gain the necessary experience while being able to effectively target your customer base. Then, you can expand your outreach once your business is up and running.

When advertising your business, consider contacting local apartment buildings, senior care facilities, as well as placing classified ads in your local newspaper. You could also contact day care services, and anywhere else that you can think of that would require regular cleaning services.

Start Your Own Business Today!

Consider printing business cards and distributing them everywhere you go. From local gas stops, shopping malls, hair salons to restaurants, you can effectively get your message out without spending a lot of money in advertising.

You should also print out half page advertisements rather than just business cards and post your flyers throughout your neighborhood. You could consider hiring a couple of teenagers to distribute your marketing message by posting them on signs, public service boards, on car windshields and on bulletin boards.

Take a grassroots approach to marketing your business and you'll be able to build a solid client base while saving a lot of money along the way!

You should also consider listing your new business in the local yellow pages and other business directories that will help maximize exposure and build a client list.

If you have the marketing budget, you could purchase air time via your local radio station, or take out an advertisement in your classifieds (which is often more affordable).

Make sure to highlight the benefits of your cleaning service as well as provide a direct contact line so potential clients can easily contact you with questions. Your ad doesn't have to include a listing of all of your service options but instead, the most important (and popular) ones.

Do not include your rates within your advertisements!

Let people call you to discuss what they need and base your prices on a per-client basis, as each home will be different and every client will require different services.

The cleaning service isn't a "one size fits all" business, and you need to communicate your message to potential clients that you are willing to create an affordable cleaning service plan, just for them!

Last minute tips:

Contact your local Chamber of Commerce for licensing information regarding your home based cleaning business. You should be able to get started with a simple business registration, which can cost anywhere between $50 and $120 per year.

Shop at wholesale distributors like Costco, as well as janitorial supply centers so that you can save money by purchasing cleaners and supplies in bulk. Keep an eye on weekly flyers, looking for discounts and savings wherever you can!

While being "bonded" isn't usually required for residential cleaning, if you plan to include commercial buildings in your cleaning service, you will want to become registered and bonded.

Contact your local business center for information on how to proceed as well as overall costs involved. You want to leave yourself plenty of time to take care of everything before launching your new cleaning service to the public!

Purchase a cell phone and pager (unless your cell phone as texting service) and include the number on your business cards and flyers so that interested parties can contact you quickly. You want to make it as easy as possible so that you can cater to busy families and professionals.

Set up a voice mail system to collect calls when you are not available, and return calls promptly, even if you are full and are not accepting new clients, you should still follow up with everyone who calls, offering to place them on your waiting list. It's a great way to secure clients for when your business expands!

Spend time creating a quote spreadsheet that can be easily adjusted based on a client's requests and preferences.

You want to include your business name, contact information, and service outline when submitting bids for client work. Attach a business card to your quote sheet when distributing to potential clients.

• **Cake Decorating Business**

The cost of starting your own cake decorating business is a lot less than you might think, especially when compared to more traditional brick and mortar businesses. Since your first step should be to create a service from your home you can save on overhead costs, such as rental space, larger equipment and of course, staff.

To start your business from home you will just need the essentials including basic equipment, baking supplies and of course elbow room! You should also designate an area that you use for your baking supplies.

Extra storage space goes a long way in this business, believe me!

How should you begin?

My first step was decorating birthday cakes for families in my community. I placed a few ads in the local classified and put up some bulletins on the shopping mall entrance boards.

Within a few days I had calls from potential clients, and within a week I had over 11 orders. I catered to baby and bridal showers as well. These cakes will be the main source of your income at first, however as you grow and take on the wedding industry you will see your business really soar! Personally I focused on birthday cakes at first, until I honed and improved my skills.

While every cake is very important wedding cakes tend to be the center point of the event, since it is a very large part of the reception process. In addition, wedding cakes are highly photographed especially as the newlyweds cut into it. For this reason I treaded carefully and only focused on wedding events after I had been in business for a couple of months. As a cake decorator you must realize your responsibilities are enormous.

If you are confident in your craft, I encourage you to accept wedding clients right from the start, however if you aren't, do as I did and start off catering to smaller events because once word gets out that people enjoy your cakes, you will be stunned at how many orders you will receive! Please don't be intimidated by the importance of a wedding cake. Every single baker in our situation is nervous as heck at first. I can't tell you how many cakes I destroyed attempting to get it perfect the first few times.

Skill comes with time and if you believe in yourself and your abilities, you will develop a style that is unique and just as good as some of the most world renowned in the industry. In addition if practice makes perfect, you will have lots of that soon enough!

Without a doubt there is a huge market for beautifully decorated cakes however in the early phase of your career you will be required to do a great deal of self-advertising. This can be time consuming and in some cases, you might get bored of the repetitive aspect of it all but once this footwork has been done, it will be so much easier to continually market yourself. Developing your own brand (and reputation) is the first step in introducing your new service to your community.

A good promotional strategy will help you focus on your current market, get the most out of your advertising efforts and ensure that a consistent, high quality image is maintained.

You want to get the word out quickly and as affordably as possible while ensuring you are still effectively targeting your potential customers properly, right?

Perhaps you have heard that marketing your product is the key to success in any business, cakes or otherwise. So, to create the best advertising campaigns that you can you have to put yourself in the shoes of the customer you are targeting. This is the very fundamental of marketing regardless of what industry you are in.

You must ask yourself a few important questions such as:

Why would a customer come to me and not a competitor? What am I offering that is unique? What discounts, coupons, special incentives can I offer my potential customers to jump start my business by having them give me a chance, rather than continuing to go to the local bakery?

How can I stand out? What can I do differently that a customer would appreciate? (Faster turnaround times perhaps, free birthday card package if it's a birthday cake you are decorating, etc.).

Your promotional package should highlight the benefits of using your service, and showcase why you are different. You have to stand out in order to gain as many new customers as possible.

Simple things can make a huge impact on how your customers view you. As suggested above, if you are decorating a birthday cake, throwing in a free package of candles or a bag of balloons is low cost but different.

Put your own personal touch on your packages and you will see incredible results.

I took the "grass route" method when marketing my business because I didn't have a huge advertising budget to work with.

I had to be innovative and figure out how to reach as many people as possible the most affordable way that I could. It would have been far easier if I had the ability to broadcast on the radio, or set up ads on our local community channel but in my case, that wasn't possible when I first started. Since I had such a restricted budget I paid particular attention to every single method I used to ensure that I didn't waste resources on the things that weren't really yielding any new sales. Here are some of the ways that I advertised my cake decorating business.

Local Newspaper Advertisements

It cost me $40 to run an ad for two months in my local newspaper. I then branched out to cover newspapers in other communities because my ad was so effective that I was then generating revenue from my decorating business to cover the cost of additional ads. The first step is to create a list of every newspaper in your area (and surrounding areas if you are in a smaller city or town).

Find out if they have a website if possible because if so, it makes the process even easier and faster. Once you have your list, find out what their ad prices are. Target the ones that are more affordable at first, because even though they may have a smaller readership, you can see how effective your ads are (and if they need tweaking) without spending a lot of money.

When you advertise choose the longest available campaign that you can to make sure it runs (and it seen) by as many people as possible.

One ad, one time will not yield nearly as much as if people see your ad multiple times, a proven strategy that Internet marketing gurus have tested throughout the years. In fact, they say it takes the average person four times viewing an ad before they remember it.

My Ads Went Zoom

I know it might sound tacky but because I was on a shoestring budget I decided to try out the car magnet idea. It worked like a charm and didn't cost me that much at all. Just make sure that you have a website before you try this technique because people will NOT remember your phone number. They are far more likely to remember your website address instead.

Refrigerator Magnets

Turn your business card into a refrigerator magnet.

The magnets can be given to each customer when they pick up their cake (along with other "plain" business cards to give to the guests at their party).

Bridal Gown and Tux Shops

Visit bridal gown and tuxedo shops in your area and request permission to display your business cards on their counter top or bulletin board. Purchase inexpensive, clear cardholders in which to display your cards. Ask the shop owner for permission to display a beautifully decorated dummy wedding cake in their store.

Other Wedding Vendors

Speak to the owners of other shops in your area that cater to the wedding and special events industry.

Ask about placing your business cards in a prominent location in their shops and possibly creating a display similar to the one described above, using their items along with a bridal cake. Also ask about collaborative advertising in the newspaper.

Other businesses to consider include hair salons, nail salons, day spas, jewelry stores, etc.

Other Places for Cards and Displays

Below are other businesses and groups that you might consider asking for permission to display business cards:

- Children's party places and hosted events
- Sports Events Craft Stores
- Daycare Providers
- Beauty Salons (I got a lot of business from these)
- Baby stores (baby showers always have cake!)
- Lingerie Shops (or anywhere else that brides-to-be go)

Just remember there is no shop that has customers that won't need your services.

If you are a bake regularly you probably already have most of these baking tools in your kitchen, however if you don't, rest assured that most of the baking supplies are relatively inexpensive, and some of them can be purchased at a later date whenever you receive a custom order that requires them since otherwise they aren't used that often. Here are the tools that I made sure I had when I started my cake decorating business.

A heavy-duty mixer is a must. This will quickly become your new best friend. It's an essential piece of equipment for the cake decorator and something you cannot avoid buying.

The Kitchen Aid 5 quart Artisan stand mixer is perfect for the job. They are not cheap however they will save you a lot of time, so it's well worth the investment. If you shop around you can usually find them on sale, so be sure to hunt down a bargain for this item before you buy one.

Cake Turntable

Sturdy turntables are a necessity. There are several styles and designs available for the sugar artist. There are many sizes, designs and prices to choose from. A better quality turntable is best since that way when you get into heavier tiered cakes you will not have to purchase a new turntable.

Baking Pans

Good quality basic shaped pans. As you are acquiring your equipment buy the best quality pans you can afford.

Buying good pans does make a difference. Don't buy the bargain versions if you plan on using them for a long time. Multiple sets of the basic shape pans will allow you to bake in a shorter amount of time. One 14" pan must cool after baking before you can wash it, refill it and bake again.

Note: Measure the inside of your oven before buying the larger size pans. The other shapes such as hexagon, square, rectangular and etc. are not requested as often in the wedding cake business so I only keep 2 sets of each of those.

Versatile Shaped Pans - The ball, petite doll pan, horseshoe, and others can be used for many things. The ball pan can be used for all kinds of balls, soccer, basketball, baseballs, and etc.

Half of the ball pan can be used for a baseball cap, a domed top on a building, or maybe even rounded top on a wedding cake. That little pan is very versatile.

Make sure the pans you purchase have 90-degree sides and corners. If you will be doing cheesecakes, purchase pans with removable sides.

- Cooling racks
- Large heavy duty cooling racks are a necessity.
- Separators

As your business grows and you start to create wedding cakes you will need separators.

Choose wisely in deciding on the type of separators you want to use. The most stable of set ups is the type that the legs go through the cake and rest on the plate below. Again storage space is important along with the look you want.

- Angled spatula - For applying and smoothing icing.
- Piping (or pastry) bags – For creating borders and other decorations.
- Couviers - For changing tips easily.

- Digital Camera A really good camera. Learn to take really good close up pictures of your cakes. When you are trying to establish yourself in your community as a sugar artist these pictures will show your customers just what you can do.

Other Items to remember:

- Greaseproof paper
- Tissue paper
- Foil
- Icing scraper or comb
- Icing ruler or comb
- Serrated knife
- Decoration for top of cake
- Pillars (if required)

When you are really ready to make a go of cake decorating as a business, you need to determine exactly what you can afford to invest and stay within your budget.

Typically the biggest investment you will need to make is in an electric mixer.

Once you complete your research and purchase a mixer, you will probably also realize that there are a host of other wonderful items that could be used in your decorating business.

When getting started with a cake decorating business, there are so many things to remember and so many documents to keep track of. Be sure to set aside space in your house in addition to your kitchen, specifically for the business.

The tax advantages may be significant when operating a home Office. A cake decorating business really isn't the kind of business that requires a storefront, at least in the early stages. As you grow, you may want to consider that route.

A home office does not have to be glamorous, but it does need to be exclusively used for business and it does need to be comfortable.

CHAPTER 4- BUSINESSES THAT YOU CAN START ALMOST IMMEDIATELY (WITH SPACE REQUIRED)

• **Daycare Service**

If you enjoy children and have the patience and creativity needed, a home based childcare and day care service might be the perfect business for you! Child care providers play an important role in the lives of busy parents who need a reliable and honest person to care for their children while they are working or away. If you can demonstrate your ability to properly care for children, you'll find it very easy to build your client base with little advertising involved.

The first step is to take a good look around your home. Are you prepared to make significant changes in order to accommodate room for playtime as well as to ensure that the environment is safe?

When it comes to parents evaluating a childcare provider for their children, one of their greatest concerns is whether their children will be adequately cared for while being free to roam and play without potential danger. You will also need to secure a business license in order to watch children in your home and in certain areas; you may also be required to complete a background check in order to demonstrate that you are a responsible person who is able to care for small children. One of the most decisions you'll make will be in choosing the age demographic for your childcare service. It's always best to focus on a specific age group rather than accept children of all different ages so that you can develop a routine and schedule that effectively accommodates the needs of children in a specific age group.

For example, caring for toddlers requires a great deal more effort and energy than caring for pre-teens who don't require as much room to play. Furthermore, the age demographic will also play a factor in the number of children you can adequately care for, with younger children requiring more attention and monitoring than older children. The startup costs associated with running a daycare service is minimal.

Apart from safety precautions, you will only need to purchase supplies to keep children occupied, as well as develop a healthy meal plan and daily snacks. It's important that you demonstrate your commitment to providing a safe and fun environment for children by developing an activity schedule that provides the fundamental building blocks that help prepare children for school, as well as to bolster their creativity.

It's important to parents that their children are able to learn throughout the day, to get exercise and fresh air rather than being kept indoors watching television, so the more you focus on developing an activity schedule that offers them the opportunity to evaluate what their children will be doing from day to day, and the more enjoyable you make their time with you, the easier it will be to retain long term clients who know that their children are in good hands!

The cost of supplies should be factored into your daily rates, and to accommodate short-term daycare sessions, you should create a price plan that caters to parents who require day-to-day childcare as well as parents who only need childcare every so often.

You need to be reasonable with the number of children that you can adequately care for and again, pay special attention to age groups. It's often easier to care for a larger number of children who are close in age than to care for children whose ages are very different.

You also want to check in with any local regulations that restrict the number of children that you are allowed to care for at any given time, and make sure that your home can handle the number of children that you are considering caring for.

Consider hiring a helper or assistant who can take over when you need to step out. This is very important if you plan on caring for a larger number of children.

You could also consider developing an after-school program where you can pick up children from school and care for them until their parents are home from work.

This is a very high demand service and if you are able to demonstrate your ability and commitment to properly care for children, you will find it very easy to secure enough clients to go forward with your business.

• Hair and Nail Specialist

The hair and nail salon industry is booming with reports of over $4.2 billion dollars in sales predicted for the upcoming year! Regardless of the economy, people continue to have their nails and hair done so this is not only a profitable market to get involved in, but also an evergreen market.

The cost of a haircut and manicure will vary depending on the area so your first step is to evaluate the competition to determine an appropriate price structure for your hair and nail salon.

You want to make sure your prices are reasonable so that you don't turn away potential clients, while being careful not to limit your profit potential. Of course, your pricing will depend on a number of factors including: Your local area – Do you live in a high end area of the city where people are more accustomed to paying $50 for a haircut?

Your specialty – Are you able to offer additional services or extended features such as hair straightening, hair relaxants and treatments? Competition – What is the competition in your area charging for similar services? How can you take a new approach to your business to highlight your services and optimize pricing?

Your Hours – You can charge more per session if your business offers "after hours" or "in house" sessions where you travel to your clients home or business to complete the treatment. Determining your price structure requires careful research and market evaluation. Setting your prices too high will minimize business while setting your prices too low will hinder your ability to generate a healthy profit.

When setting your pricing consider all overhead costs, including supplies, travel expenses, labor costs and overhead. It's reasonable to estimate that your overhead costs will be from 30-40% of your labor and cost of supplies.

You also want to check with your local business office to determine what business zoning, licenses or guidelines may affect your ability to run a home based business. In addition, since you will be offering services in your home, you will need to set up an area of your house devoted to your business.

Not only will this help you develop a professional presence in your area, but a percentage of all costs associated with running your business will be tax deductible, and it's important to properly manage and maintain a separation between your household and the area in which your business takes place. You could also consider renting space in an office building or local shopping mall if you feel it's affordable and easier to set up. There are advantages to having an actual storefront including the fact that you'll have "built in business" from traffic and customers who discover your business when at the mall or shopping plaza.

While there is no requirement that you complete training in order to offer hair cutting and styling services, you will need a license in order to perform manicures. When it comes to making money in the hair and nail business, it's all about the numbers. You need to carefully consider your hours of operation so that you can maximize the number of clients that come through your doors, but you should also consider "extended" services to cater to those who work longer shifts or are unable to book in sessions throughout the day. Not only will this help you establish yourself as a flexible service focusing on your client, but you will be able to generate business just by including customers that traditional business hours leave out.

You should also keep in mind that the more specialized your services are, the better. While the hair and nail salon will always be in demand throughout the year, there are seasonal influences that you need to include in your business plan. For example, during the summer months you're likely to receive bookings for weddings, and in the winter months, people are often interested in more frequent cutting and styles for the holiday season, concerts and festive events.

When setting up your home based business, you'll need proper equipment in order to run your hair and nail salon, including:

Dryers Straighteners Brushes and Combs Curling Iron Color services (dyes, glazing, highlights, streaks)

Hair treatments (scalp treatments, relaxers etc.) If you are planning to include nail and foot care into your service menu, you'll also need: Nail wrapping Acrylic nail applications Polish and lacquer Paraffin treatment supplies Sculpted nail applications

Appointment books and receipts are also a necessity. Finally, getting a business telephone number is a necessary step in setting yourself up as a professional in your field.

Depending on the extent of your services you may require additional supplies and equipment so it's important to carefully plan out your service menu to determine what supplies you will need as well as what kind of services are currently in demand in your area.

• Pet Sitting Service

Pet owners are a great market to cater to because they're willing to do just about anything to make sure that their pets are adequately cared for. Going out of town? They need a pet sitter to attend to their beloved friend, and a home based pet sitting business is often more appealing than dropping their pet off at a kennel where their pet is often boarded without personal care or exercise, while being crowded in with other animals for days on end. So, how can you start a successful pet sitting home-based business?

It's easy! If you have a love of furry creatures and you don't mind long walks, a dog sitting business might be your true calling. When creating a pet sitting business, you can choose to offer "in house" sitting where you visit your clients' home and care for their animals while they are away at work or on a trip, or you can offer to care for their pets at your own home, which is often the more preferred option.

Pet sitting involves a number of services including:

- Overnight care
- Walking
- Grooming And Bathing
- Feeding
- Playing
- Giving pets medications and creams

The startup costs are minimal as the only supplies you'll need will be a leash, collars (in multiple sizes), food and play toys, although most pet owners will prefer to provide all of this to you as they'll want their pets to stay on a consistent meal plan with certain brand name foods that they are used to.

Furthermore, for safety precautions it's always best to ask the pet owners for play toys, chains, collars and walking leashes so that you are using their own supplies and equipment, suitable for their pet.

When developing your business, you will want to thoroughly evaluate your options, keeping in mind that there are many different types of pets you could offer care for.

For example, if you are fond of cats, you could offer a cat sitting service instead. There are also people looking for someone to drop by and feed and care for their birds, rabbits, and fish as well!

Whatever you decide, be careful not to offer sitting services for different animals on the same day. Certain breeds don't play well together, and you need to keep this in mind when developing your business. If you plan to attend to pets at your home, you may want to consider investing in proper fencing so that you are able to let dogs run and play without concern of them getting out into traffic or being lost.

And finally, make sure to communicate with local pet owners who are your potential clients. You want to know what is most important to them, what type of services are in most demand as well as what they don't want you to do (certain owners may not want you to provide treats, walk dogs in certain areas, etc.).

Pet owners are very protective of their furry friends and they want them to be cared for by service providers in the same way that they would personally care for them, so it's important that you understand the mindset of your clients by taking the time to discuss their concerns and questions before developing your business. If you listen to what future clients want before going too far into preparing for your home based business, you'll be able to

Start Your Own Business Today!
use this valuable information to create a tailor-made pet sitting business that is bound to be a hit!

Note: If you keep pets in your own home, your local area may require some sort of licensing. Be sure to check your local laws before you begin to see if you need any type of special licensing.

Chapter 5- How to Overcome the Emotional Dynamics in Investing

Investing can be an emotional roller coaster for many people. This holds true whether you are investing in real estate, gold, the stock market, your own business, or whatever you consider your investments to be. There are some basic things you can do to make the process less emotional and in turn, less stressful. Make sure you do not over-extend yourself, be aware of when your break even points may be, and have a back-up plan if your first plan doesn't work the way you thought it would.

Do Not Over-Extend Yourself

There is one main reason that over extending yourself financially for an investment is never a good idea. It does not allow for any error, change, or learning curve. Most often people rely on others to participate in some way to make their investments successful. Most businesses need people to run it, investment properties need tenants, and market investors need professionals to guide them. If somebody lets you down it will be hard to bounce back if you are over extended.

The Break Even Point Different

Investments have different break even points. If you are looking to break even quickly and start being fully profitable you are likely looking at investments that are not as risky. Higher risk equals higher reward. Lower risk equals less reward. A combination of both investments is excellent to have. After you have reached a breakeven point you open up your investments to valuable other opportunities too.

A Plan for the Plan

At first thought that probably sounds ridiculous but it is necessary. One of the most stressful things that can happen to investors is to not have things go the way they envisioned. Creating a plan in the first place will allow you to realistically evaluate your expectations and investments. No solid plan should be all or nothing. That is when the back-up plan comes in to play for investors. It allows you the flexibility to make adjustments and tweaks when necessary.

The dynamics of investing can be very emotional and stressful if not properly managed. When you are aware of what is all involved you give yourself the power to avoid those situations or at least manage them effectively. That will make your investments more exciting, rewarding, and enjoyable. Those positive factors will only lead to greater success in all that achieve with investments and life.

Aim for Well-Rounded Investment Plans

If you want to be a solid investor you will find that you need one critical component. That component is a diversified portfolio. Diversified portfolios help ensure that you will have balance and risk management considerations in place for your portfolio. Experienced investors and financial advisors have discovered the significant importance of diversification for increasing financial gain and reducing loss. The concept is simple. You need to have a well-rounded portfolio that has a variety of high risk to low risk investments. That way, if one does great you are ahead. On the other hand, if one does not go great you are not behind. The three main categories of investments you need to balance out in your portfolio are cash, stocks, and bonds.

Diversifying these three things in your portfolio will make it strong and give it the best chances of working effectively for you.

Cash

Cash is the portion of your assets that should be considered the most liquid. That doesn't mean you tap into it whenever you have the desire to do so. It means that you have access to it if you need it for a major purchase. Most people choose options such as Certificates of Deposit and Money Market accounts for this part of their portfolio. It provides flexibility, low or non-existent penalties for withdrawals, and the opportunity to earn some interest on the money.

Stocks

When you are starting an investment portfolio or adjusting a current one stock is the first item to address. Out of the three investment areas, stocks are the most volatile and require the most diversification. When it comes to stocks there are not only high risk and low risk, but also small caps and large caps. You need to do your research or find a financial advisor to help research for you with this one. There are diversified portfolio options now that even tie in with your personal beliefs and help you support the causes you consider important.

Bonds

Bonds are a unique investment because they have an end date and a guaranteed interest rate. Governments, municipalities, and corporations are the most frequent users of bonds. When you start looking into bonds you will hear the term blue chip. A blue chip bond is one that is considered less risky. The best way to tell if a bond is high or low risk is the interest rate that it offers. The lower the rate of return the more stable the bond is considered. Higher rates of return are associated with higher risk.

Chapter 6- Real Estate is Still the Best Investment

The housing market may not be in the best condition ever right now. Let's face it, the market appears to be about as bad as it can get. What is important to remember is that it is not bad for everybody. Buyers have a wonderful opportunity to purchase a home that is a good investment. Here are seven reasons why purchasing a home now is not a bad idea.

1. The selection. The homes that are on the market right now are fairly extensive in many areas. You will have a broader range of homes to consider in your price range than what has been available in a long time.

2. The value. The value of homes has gone down in all markets over the past years. With lending restrictions being implemented and financial industry woes the same amount of people do not qualify for purchasing homes unless they have a substantial down payment. That is one big reason that the supply has went up. You can get more of a home at a lesser price.

3. Tax deductions. When you own a home you open up the opportunity to receive several tax benefits that are not available to you as a renter. You can deduct interest, taxes, energy efficiency upgrades, and more. There is nobody that could tell you all your possibilities aside from a tax accountant.

4. Express yourself. When you own your home it opens up the possibilities that you may enjoy for decorating, landscaping, playing, and having fun. Depending on the type of home you could finally have that space to decorate with that perfect color or start gardening if you have a yard. The only limit is your imagination.

5. Always in demand. People will always need to have a place to live. They will most always be interested in purchasing too. Despite a tough economy right now you will have people looking at your home down the road if you choose to sell it.

6. Appreciation. Yes, your home will ideally appreciate in value but the appreciation I am speaking of is the type of appreciation that goes with owning something. When you own something as substantial as a house you feel proud. You are most likely to take care of your investment because it may be with you a long time.

What to Consider When Investing in Real Estate

Investment properties have long been considered a way to create an investment opportunity that will provide long term financial benefits. We all know that the real estate market has been in turmoil the past years and that is expected to continue for a while. That does not mean that it is not a good time to consider purchasing investment properties however.

Here are seven things to consider and be aware of if you are interested in purchasing residential investment properties.

• Can you collect the amount of rent that will offset the mortgage payment and expenses? Ideally you can, but if you cannot you need to make sure that you have the additional income to offset the monthly payments and expenses associated with the property. Even if you have to chip in some of your funds every month to offset you could still end up ahead.

• Do you have the time to devote to being a landlord? Investment properties do not just take care of themselves. Like any residence, unexpected repairs and emergencies to arrive with investment properties. You need to make sure that you are available or you have somebody available to tend to those situations immediately.

• Is your city landlord friendly? Some cities are completely into the rights of tenants and very negligent of the rights of landlords. You need to make sure you understand and accept the criteria for investment properties that are set forth by the city.

• Will a vacancy bankrupt your wallet? Investment properties need to have reserves tied to them. It would be perfect and ideal if you had the next tenant waiting as one left. That is seldom the case though. Make sure you can swing the months when you do not have a tenant.

•How long would you like to keep the investment property? It seldom pays to own an investment property for just a few years. The real gain comes from long term ownership. Make sure that you understand the tax and investment consequences of owning investment properties.

•Can you treat your investment property like a business? When you are in the business of providing people their residential homes you need to be able to take a business stance when they throw personal reasons at you. It is sad when people have hardships and don't make their payments, but it is not your responsibility or goal to cover them. They probably will not catch up.

Consider Every Investment Well

Investing can be daunting and intimidating for some people. Lately, the whole subject of investing has received a lot of attention. If you are just getting started with investing or revamping your prior investment strategies you need to make sure that you are wise with your decisions and do not compromise on them. That takes some discipline. Three things you can do to help maintain your discipline are to create a plan, separate your emotions, and be patient.

Create a Plan

Investing requires a plan just like any other business adventure. An investment plan should consider how to make your investments well rounded, an investment budget that you can stick to, and the results you expect.

•A well rounded plan will make sure that all your options are not riding on one factor.

•Make sure you are being realistic with your investment budget. It is not practical to think that you can invest 50% of all your income each and every month in long term investments. You need to have access to emergency funds that don't have a penalty or fee attached to them.

•Evaluate your desired results with your investment plan. The market and earning money from it takes time. You should not expect to see huge gains monthly or even yearly.

Your Emotions are Not Included in Your Business

Our finances are every bit as much an emotional topic as a business one. When the market takes a down swing and you see hard earned money go away you must remember that it is temporary. That is not always easy to do. History is on your side though. The past trends have shown that people do gain when they invest in the stock market overall. That happens with time, dedication, and perseverance.

Be Patient

Patience is not only a virtue but it is vital when you are investing. Watching your money shrink and grow can be difficult. Make sure you have some systems in place for managing your patience. You may want to consider not looking at market performance daily and evaluating the overall picture once a month. That will help keep your sanity. In turn, you and your loved ones will be much happier and less stressed as a result. Create a plan, separate your emotions, and be patient when you invest. When you do those three things you will find investing to be fun, exciting, and less stressful.

Chapter 7- Other Attractive Investment Opportunities You Can Try

• **Mutual Funds**

A mutual fund is a way to have a well-diversified investment within one opportunity. You pool your funds in with others that choose to participate in that mutual fund and the result can be an excellent rate of return. Here are seven reasons why many people consider mutual funds an attractive investment alternative.

1. The wide variety of mutual funds available allow for many options and solid options. There are mutual funds that invest into blue chip (proven companies). They are considered fairly safe and secure because they are lower risk.

2. Mutual funds are fairly liquid. You can set up an open end mutual fund and receive funds quickly. You can have a closed end mutual funds and receive funds down the road. It is nice to know

that you have options. Many people like open end because they can act more quickly if a new opportunity comes along.

3. Many mutual funds have a smaller cost of transaction.

4. Investment professionals manage mutual funds. That gives investors the assurance of an expert working for them. It also can help relieve stress because you pay a small fee to know that somebody is watching your money as carefully as you would.

5. Mutual funds are highly regulated. Those regulations make it easy to track daily change and movement of your mutual fund. When you can easily track how your mutual fund is doing you can prepare for possible adjustments you may consider making or just enjoy watching your excellent investment prosper.

6. Mutual funds have a fairly high rate of return and the process of cashing them in is fairly simple. First you can pay yourself and then you can take care of paying the other things that you need to with the proceeds. You can also shift from one fund to another within the same family.

7. Mutual funds are fairly diversified. That means that if one portion of it is weak the other portions can help lift you back up and off-set any losses. That type of risk management is very appealing for the mutual fund investor.

Investment is not risk free. Mutual funds are one great way to decrease loss while still having a diversified investment plan. Make sure you check out how a mutual fund could be beneficial to you.

Investments for a College Degree

As a parent you have every reason to be very proud of your child for wanting to go to college and getting accepted into the college of their choice. Most parents also want to help pay for their children's education and need to find out how to make their money really work for them. There are two things that all parents can agree upon. Kids grow way too fast and going to college is expensive. As a parent, you do not want to make the mistake of procrastinating when it comes to saving for your child's (or children's) education. Here are a few of the best investments you can make that are designed to help your children go to the college they want and not have as much in student loans when they are done.

• Traditional investment options.

The traditional investment options are savings accounts, taxable investment accounts, annuities, and U.S. Savings Bonds. These have long been popular options for parents to use when saving for their children's education. They provide stability and a great rate of return.

• Section 529 College Savings Programs.

Section 529 programs are operated by states or educational institutions to help parents set aside funds for their children to go to college. Every state has at least one 529 program available. The thing that really makes the 529 attractive to parents starting to save for college now are that they can live in one state, invest in another states 529 program and their child can go to college in an entirely different state. That flexibility is reassuring and it also plays a great role in keeping various 529's competitive and profitable for those who invest in them.

• Coverdell Education Savings Account.

This account was formerly called an Education IRA. The strength of a Coverdell Education Savings Account is that you invest in it with after tax dollars. When it is time to withdraw funds for education you will need to meet a few criteria but will most likely have a tax free, penalty free withdrawal for college expenses.

With increasing education costs more viable savings options for college have come to be. Parents know that they need to make college financial considerations for their children from the time they are infants to prepare. Eighteen years can go very quickly and it is important to be ready.

• Foreign Exchange

There are two options available to people investing in the Foreign Exchange market. The more common name for this market is Forex. When you do decide to invest in Forex you is either investing in the US Dollar or the Euro. Both currencies have their own set of pro's and con's. Make sure you learn the differences before you decide to dive into this type of investing.

The Pros of Investing In the US Dollar

• You can intentionally drive the US Dollar value down. While that may sound negative it is positive for making US export has a more attractive price for buyers from foreign markets.

• If US exports are driving a lower price it leads to narrowing the margin for the US trade deficit.

• Historically, Canada has always profited from purchasing the US Dollar. In fact, it is one way that many people earn money on the

Forex market with a simple technique. Depending on bank or ATM fees you can just do currency swaps yourself through credit cards or your personal accounts.

The Cons of Investing In the US Dollar

•A weaker US Dollar often leads to other countries trying to weaken their currency against it. That is one way they protect their trade market.

•Weak US Dollars on a global scale lead to higher oil prices. We all know the negative impact of that in the long run.

•A weak US Dollar may decrease the trade deficit but it does nothing to help another important deficit – our national debt.

The Pros of Investing In the Euro

•When there is a stronger foreign currency rate the US Dollar thrives. Our rate becomes stronger at the same time. When the Euro dollar is strong it will be beneficial for your Forex trading and investment.

•The Euro is the official currency in twenty two countries now. That gives people the benefit of the Euro being strong from a diverse set of economies and also makes it the accepted currency of many countries if you are a frequent traveler. The Cons of Investing In the Euro

•It is difficult to make it profitable if you do not get an exchange rate that is close to the rate of the US Dollar.

•The amount of options available for trading Euro makes it overwhelming to investors at times.

ABOUT THE AUTHOR

Jeff White is an investments specialist who has become an authority when he began gracing conferences and other business events.

Jeff is married with a 5-year-old daughter, Lea. When not working, he would spend his time gardening and playing with his daughter.